The 7 Laws of Fear:

How to Make Your Deepest Insecurities Your Greatest Strengths

By C.K. Murray

Fight. Or. Flight.

Three basic words. Three basic words that form the *crux* of what the world's happiest, most successful individuals have always known. It is these three words that fuel every fighter, every go-getter, every man or woman who chases fearlessly in the direction of their dreams. These simple but powerful words that bring the strong to their thrones, and the weak to their knees.

So how do *you* respond? Have you ever stood face to face with that very person, place or thing that makes you quiver? Have you ever challenged yourself to overcome your greatest fears, the greatest source of your doubts and insecurities?

How often have *you* confronted the biggest obstacles in your life?

Chances are, you're afraid. It doesn't happen all the time, and it doesn't happen wherever you go. But it does happen. And truth be told, it's hurting you.

So stop with the excuses. Stop existing in a bubble, stop

fleeing or avoiding those things that challenge you or make you uncomfortable. Stop selling yourself an endless line of reasons for you mediocrity, for your inability to conquer what others have and do.

Stop living your life in fear!

It is time to transform...

Success is what you make it.

You don't have to be a multimillionaire to be successful, just as you don't have to spend every day living paycheck to paycheck to be *un*successful. True success stems from an ability to know two things: (1) that you have satisfied your basic needs, and (2) that you have provided yourself, and those you care about, the room and time for personal freedom. This means the license to pursue passions, to exercise creativity, to navigate morals, and to engage in problem-solving. Without personal freedom, true success can never be attained.

Another reason for lack of success, is a lack of self-awareness. Too often, people fail to be successful because they fail to truly find what makes them tick. They lack emotional intelligence. They never fully grasp what it is that inspires them, motivates them, keeps them feeling young and happy, significant and valuable. More often than not, the average Joe will slink through life accepting things as good enough, even when such 'things' are far from what's desired.

So then what happens?

Simple. If a person continues along the path of mediocrity, existing but not living, life in total begins to lose its value. Everyday events become bland and colorless. You may tell yourself that you're content, that you're comfortable, but the truth is more haunting. Many times, the only reason we feel comfortable is because we've never been *un*comfortable. We've settled. We've accepted one way of life in a world of 8 billion people, on a planet spanning 25,000 miles around, with nearly 200 countries, over 4,000 cities, and enough variety and versatility to make even the most imaginative humans jump with joy...

For most people, settling is the status quo. We find our bubble, and we rarely bother to expand.

Settling is a result of fears, doubts and insecurities that lead us to give up on being as happy as we could, or should. When we settle, we lose track of what matters. Even worse, we forget what excites. Moments of triumph go unnoticed and the hours, days, weeks, months and years of life meld together. In the end, the potential for happiness and security is replaced by a deep, heavy, unending haze.

Get up, go to work, get home, go to sleep. Rinse and repeat. And so the cycle continues…

But what if it doesn't have to? What if you can conquer all your fears, if you can use those very fears to propel yourself in entirely new directions? To claim success and personal freedom once and for all? To carve the life you want without regret? What if—lo and behold—your deepest, most crippling fears and insecurities are actually your closest friends?

Doubtful? Good, then that means you're thinking…

So let's put that thinking to use!

Law 1 — You Only Fail When You Stop Trying

Too many people are terrified of messing up.

But even worse, too many people are terrified of admitting they're terrified of messing up. So what do they do? Easy, they lie. They put up a shell. They hide the truth, stretch the facts, and avoid coming to grips with their own demons.

Instead of going after what what they want deep down inside, they suppress it. They tell themselves that something isn't worth doing because they're not good at it. They tell themselves that a task is too long, too hard, too far outside their range. They feed themselves a load of horseshit so that they don't feel bad; so that they have a 'reason' for being less than they could.

Truth be told, it's a common practice, and one that gets us nowhere.

The reason so many people give up prematurely, or don't try at all, is because of that little thing called 'failure.' When we think of failure, we think of weakness. We imagine not paying our bills on time, never reaching our dreams, never getting the girl or guy, woman or man, wife or husband that we covet. By and large, failure denotes finality. It denotes an end to what was once a gleaming possibility; it represents an inability to get what we want.

And, boy oh boy, does that inability haunt us.

But why? Why do so many people crawl through life afraid of ghosts and demons? What is it that causes a person to break down and give up because of so-called 'failure'?

The answer is simple.

The average person does not see the truth. In truth, failure is neither good nor bad. Failure is merely an inevitable step in every process. Whether dating new people, working through school, work, or some other life trial or tribulation, failure is as normal and ubiquitous as air.

Think of all the times you've struggled. All the instances in which you didn't immediately succeed or get something on the first try. Do you consider these failures? Did you consider small things, like learning to ride a bike and falling over, a failure? Did you consider not getting a 100% on a test a 'failure'?

The reason for these questions is obvious. Depending upon who you are and what you've lived, failure can mean anything. It can range from the smallest conceivable mistake to the largest error, such as gambling away the savings account, or losing your house or livelihood because of some transgression.

Failure can really be anything, because no person—not a single one—is flawless. In this sense, we have all failed (numerous times) and will all continue to fail (numerous times). For this reason and this reason alone, there is only one thing to do.

Fuck failure.

Forget the idea of 'failure' altogether. It's negative, counterproductive, and frankly, overused. Messing up repeatedly is not going to change if you always beat yourself up. If you consider yourself incapable, you are creating what is called a *self-fulfilling prophecy*.

It means that you expect it, so you make it happen. By thinking of yourself as a failure, you begin to try less. Your mood is dampened, your zest for life is depleted, and you generally go about things with less attention to detail, because—hey—why try? You'll still be a failure, right?

Wrong. The only time you'll be a failure is if you don't try. Failures aren't people who fight, get knocked down, and get up again. Failures are people who get knocked down and stay there. People who sulk and bitch and moan about how unfair things are, without ever making an effort to change them.

Failures give up. They resign themselves to mediocrity, shoveling convenient excuses down your throat, their throat, and the throat of any poor sap who will listen. The reason that certain people become failures is because they take the easy road.

Instead of approaching their fears, they run scared with their tails down. These are the people you've seen all over. Weak men and weak women. Neurotic messes who can't control a thing in their life and blame everything outside of them; poor, drunk or drugged-out losers who choose to numb themselves because they don't have the heart to change; average sad-sacks who once had dreams and aspirations, but now rest on their laurels, supposedly 'content' to live life forever with regret.

Failures are people who stop trying. All others, however, are not failures. People who mess up and keep doing wrong, despite trying and changing—they're not failures. And their mistakes—the many errors of their ways—are not failures. They're lessons.

Every time you can't do something the way you want it, you've learned a lesson. Whether as simple as learning that a task is difficult, or as deep as gaining some profound insight, every lesson is significant.

Life is a process, few things are made overnight. And

when they are, they often go unappreciated. This is why children born into money are predisposed to chronic boredom, behavioral issues and substance abuse. This is why men and women don't respect one another when sex comes easy. This is why people used to always getting what they want struggle with impulse control, with enjoying parts of life that are not instantly gratifying.

When we get what we want immediately, we don't value it. We have no conception of what it took to get it, or earn it. We struggle to see the point of something if that something is merely handed to us. It has no meaning and no relation to our own efforts and abilities; therefore, we expect it and we abuse it.

Again, this is why life imparts lessons. You won't learn how important it is to be on-time to your job until you've been reprimanded or fired. You won't learn what it takes to get the career of your dreams until you've struggled, been turned down, been doubted, chewed out, underutilized and undervalued. You can't know what it takes to do any x, y or z without having gone through the steps.

Step by Step, Lesson by Lesson.

You aren't failing when you don't immediately get what you want. You're learning. And with each progressive hurdle cleared, you're succeeding. You're moving further along that trajectory toward your goals and your targets. Without obstacles, we would never have the motivation to do anything.

Difficulty hardens us and gives us wisdom. Without difficulty, we atrophy. Our minds are no longer pressed and our bodies are untested.

Only the weak would choose to never strive for more. Only those who give up on their dreams are failures. All others, no matter how tireless or unsuccessful in their efforts, are learning.

Law 2 - Nobody is Better at Being YOU… Than You!

We're all guilty of it.

We wake up, with our doubts swirling about our heads, our voices louder than even the loudest talkers we know. From moment to moment, day to day, our voices linger inside us, telling us what we need to know most, and many times what we don't. When the latter occurs, it is usually pretty obvious. We tell ourselves that we are not good enough, that we don't have the ability, that we're too dumb, not good-looking enough, not deserving, not capable of exceeding somebody else. We think about how many other people we know or see who are simply 'better' at what they do than us. When we consider challenges and obstacles, it is impossible not to think of the vast number of 'better' people.

For all of us, this is a reality. But for *some* of us, this reality is all-consuming.

When we allow the thought of superior 'others' to enter our heads, we are essentially giving up our power. We are comparing ourselves out, and in doing so, we are making one critical error:

Assumption!

The problem with comparing ourselves to others is that we really, truly, don't *know* others. Sure, we have acquaintances and friends and family members and partners that we've come to understand, even people on T.V. and in the media that we *think* we understand—but how far does it go?

In most cases, comparison is a futile exercise. When we compare to others, we are not comparing our self to others… we are comparing our self to our *perception* of others. This is a crucial distinction that too many people don't realize.

Think about it. Do you really know everything about another person? Do you know how that person thinks, feels, and acts? Do you know the very thoughts that run through that person's skull when he or she, say, wakes up in the morning, or is late for work, or has a bad day, or has a great day, or stubs a toe, takes a fall, reaches up or falls down?

Do you really, truly, have any idea what being in that other person's shoes is all about? Chances are, you really don't. Chances are, you project your own thoughts and feelings onto another person. You may think that somebody dislikes you only to find out that they don't—that they really like you. You may *feel* that somebody is attracted to you, only to find out that he or she just wants to be friends. You may *believe* that somebody is confident and fearless, only to find out that beneath the convincing facade is an insecure shell of a person.

Nowadays, social media makes comparison all the more difficult. We see images of others at the beach or on vacation or out in social settings having a good time with big smiles and loud laughs. We see the various statuses and memes posted by different users, the numerous flattering and unflattering photos, the countless daily, hourly, and minute-to-minute updates of personal and social sentiment. With social media like

Facebook, Twitter, and the like, many of us are caught up in what psychologists term, *social comparison.*

Thus, it's no wonder that levels of insecurity have skyrocketed. It's no wonder that the social media age has also ushered in an age of extreme emotional instability, of narcissism, of depression, of people who live and die by the social media sword. These are the same people who stalk their Facebooks on their phones, laptops and other mobile devices. They are individuals whose hearts can shatter at one bad status, if they don't get enough likes, if they see somebody else having a better time than them. The kind of people who break into virtual arguments over nothing, who create and recreate drama to boost their own egos and feel like a necessary part of the social fabric.

Of course, none of this really matters. What people don't seem to realize is that… there's no point in constantly worrying about others!

Instead of trying to one-up somebody else, instead of existing in this fragile ego-stroking world of hypercompetition, why not let loose? Why not take a step back and realize the truth?

You *aren't* me and I'm *not* you! There will always be people who are 'better' at things. There's always going to be somebody that you or others consider smarter, better looking, faster, stronger, more funny, more witty, more dreamy, more successful, more cool, more socially adept, more popular, more camera-friendly, more powerful, more x, y and z...

The point is simple: stop trying to be somebody else!

You may wish you were this beautiful, gorgeous girl or this smart, talented handsome guy… but do you really? Do you know what he or she feels and thinks? Do you know what he or she had to go through, and continues to go through? Do you really think that just because a given person is somehow 'superior' to you, that he or she is also happier? Do you really believe that some people lead lives that are problem-free?

Here's a little secret—nobody's perfect. Not a single living soul is always happy, always content, always

capable of feeling right without worry or insecurity.
Even the most powerful, successful people have their
doubts. Their demons.

Instead of worrying about how you can somehow
compete with others, worry about yourself. Embrace
your strengths and your weaknesses. Recognize that
there is only one you, and that this 'you' is far from
ideal. You will mess up again and again, you will learn
and you will struggle, but you will also succeed. The
world isn't going to hand you a silver spoon, unless
you're among a lucky few, and even then that lucky
spoon is more harbinger of bad than good.

So be happy for who you are. Understand that it is your
quirks, your flaws, your peculiarities and idiosyncrasies
that make you uniquely you. Nobody else, as hard as
they try, will ever be you. Nobody else, as hard as they
fake it, can ever replace you.

Stop fearing failure, stop fearing the superiority of
others, stop—for goodness sake—fearing the realization
that others are somehow better than you, that you can't

do what you thought.

At the end of the day, the only voice that matters is yours. Sure, others will tell you things from time to time—maybe even all the time—but it is up to you, and you alone, to tell *yourself* where you go from there.

So love yourself, silly. You're the only *you* there will ever be...

Law 3 - It is Success, not Failure, that Scares us Most

Everybody talks about being scared of "failure."

It's embarrassing, we say; it's devastating, we feel; it leaves us believing less in ourselves in more in the power of things *outside* ourselves. We all know of fearing failure, but how many of us talk about the other side of the coin?

Fearing success?

Success is a powerful force that can bring an entirely new life to our fingertips. Success can be the gateway to feeling good, to waking up everyday with a sense of purpose and promise. If it weren't for success, or the ideal of success, nobody would have anything to live for.

Remember, success does not have to mean monetary success. Having the financial stability to do what you want is only a small part of the equation. And that's just it: *doing what you want*. Some people can never have enough money and are never happy. Others can live on a farm in the middle of nowhere and be happier than a bird with a worm.

When we are successful, we have found a life or lifestyle that is not only suitable but rewarding. We have discovered a place where fear and insecurity are replaced by an openness to life.

Unfortunately, most of us don't reach the success we desire.

And one reason we don't reach the success we desire is because we're afraid of it. Think about it. Success is scary. More than that, success is *biochemically* similar to fear. When we are afraid of something, our minds trigger the fight-or-flight mechanism in which we either flee for dear life or take the challenge on. This survival mechanism floods our bodies with numerous chemicals, hormones and neurotransmitters, jump-starting our nervous system and supercharging our mental and physical capacities. Cortisol, epinephrine, endorphins, dopamine, serotonin—you name it.

When the chain of fear is activated, it's quite literally a life and death matter.

That said, fear can also seem very much like the feelings we get with new-found success. When we first experience that breath of new success, or just a whiff of it, our bodies change. As in fear, our breathing picks up, our heart rate goes up, our sweat increases and our instincts take over. In either situation—whether outright terrified or excited/nervous for success—we will always experience an initial rush, or 'high' even, if you want to think of it in those terms.

Some people can't handle the rush.

The number one reason for fear of success is fear of new things. Success may mean that you're finally out there in the open, finally more exposed, more powerful yet also uniquely more vulnerable. There may be more demands and pressures. If you have a new job, the pay is more but so too are the expectations. If you've moved somewhere new or started a new relationship, you're scared that making things work will require *too much* work. That you'll end up ensnared in a new life you were unprepared for.

People are creatures of habit, so when something good happens, people don't know how to react. Yes, they're happy, but they're also uncertain. When we get used to something—even if that something is not objectively good or even pleasant—we become averse to change. We find familiarity in the old ways of doing things and experiencing things, and so new ways seem threatening.

Of course, embracing success can be remedied. You need only remind yourself of the things you're gaining, the things you always wanted and are now doubting. Make a list, mental notes, or some other example to serve as a reminder. Remind yourself of the increases in social esteem, the increase in money, the increase power and prestige. If your 'success' is not necessarily monetary, consider it in different terms. Remind yourself of the time you now have, the precious moments you can now saver, the memories you'll make. Maybe you finally found somebody you can love.

Maybe you've finally found a way to spend more time with your kids. Heck, maybe you deem 'success' the mere ability, the simple freedom, to do what you want. Whether success for you means having a car so you can drive to the nearest 7-11 for slurpies, or having a car that your chauffeur drives you around in—it is all about what you make it.

And if you make it a positive thing, if you see the new doors as gateways to opportunity not struggle, you've truly made it. Of course, 'making it' is only a small fragment of what really matters. Overcoming your fear of success means understanding the consequences of that success. Others may judge you. There may be more opinions, more 'experts' to tell you that you're wrong or misguided, more dissenters and haters and know-it-alls who tell you how to live your life. With success, there is always a fear of becoming somebody else. We fear that we'll suddenly transform to some shadow self, forgetting our roots and where they brought us.

We've seen it all before. Somebody finally gets what they've always wanted, but then they're somebody else.

They transform into a wastoid, or maybe a downright asshole, or an arrogant bitch, or perhaps they turn to drugs and alcohol to pass the time. Success, especially monetary success, can lead to many ugly turns and twists.

Another prominent fear of success is how it will change our 'appetites.' Once we have achieved a certain degree of success, we may want more. This is only natural. If we get used to one level of living, we may become compulsively obsessed with improving it. Take for instance, stockbrokers and business owners and other financial giants who greedily chase money after money, even when they clearly have more than enough.

When people change due to success, their values may change. This is why it's important to make a list or mental note of certain values, certain core beliefs and certain 'things' you would never allow yourself to do. Now hold yourself to this standard. Don't think of becoming successful as losing your old self but as gaining a new and improved self. It is an opportunity to explore new avenues for growth, to cultivate new skills, try on new hats, and pursue new passions. It doesn't mean that you can't occasionally revert back to old ways or enjoy lifelong hobbies. It merely means that you've added something extra to the mix.

After all, who doesn't like a cherry on top?

Law 4 - We Fear Not the Unknown, but the Uncontrolled

Many people talk about fearing the unknown. And why wouldn't they? Given everything that can happen in life, sometimes this whole living thing seems like one crap-shoot after another. At times, it seems like you don't know what you've got until it's gone, or don't know what you're getting until it hits you square in the face. Many times, life is simply random, inexplicable and unexpected.

However, that doesn't mean that there can't be meaning. Consider, for instance, the life of a devout religious person. In their mind, their eyes, life is channeled through various mediums. A higher spirit or power is handling the controls, deciding what happens and when. For religious people, faith is the crux of this outlook. With faith, everything has some significance, some meaning, which means that life's unknowns are not to be feared, but to be trusted.

Everything will work out, they say.

See, when it comes to fearing unknown, it is not the un*known* that we fear, but the un*controlled*. Think about it. There are plenty things we don't know that we don't think about, let alone fear. We fear those things that we know about it, that we are able to comprehend, even if we aren't sure of the details. The reason that we fear these things is because they make us feel scared and uncertain.

Have you ever felt like so much of your life was outside you locus of control? As if the vast majority of everyday people, places and things continued to elude your grasp? What if something happened to you or your friends or loved ones? What if there was some health mishap, or lost relationship, or death or injury or monetary downfall? What if you suddenly lost the capability to do what you had always loved or dreamed of doing?

These are the possibilities that scare us. Not the unknown, the uncontrolled. When something is outside of our control, we have to make a way to bring it back inside our circle. How do we do this?

Well, some people do it the wrong way. They become so incapacitated by their fears that they abuse drugs, numbing and destroying themselves in order to escape the all-too pressing reality of uncertainty. Other people approach life more objectively. They assess risks, they plan for the future, they try to rely on empirical evidence and hard research to determine the best course of action in any given situation. Others still just ebb and flow. They try not to control much and they let things come as they do. They reduce their stress by hoping for the best while acknowledging that bad things can and do occur.

Basically, it all depends on the person's life up to this point. The outlook hinges upon the individual's environments and background, as well as his or her **current schema**.

The important thing to remember is that not everything can be controlled. Fearing the uncontrolled means wasting time that could be spent doing other things. In order to overcome your fear of the uncontrolled, and in order to avoid becoming a neurotic control freak, it is best to be realistic. Compile a list of priorities and signal every time one is completed or met. Rank them in terms of importance and create a schedule in which you plan out steps to achieve your goals.

Hold yourself accountable. Remember, each goal should indicate something that you consider under your control. If the goal seems too lofty at first, create sub-goals that help you break down daunting tasks into their component parts. For instance, if you want to get a new job or accelerate your career, the end goal may be: *job x in 5 years*. And the sub-goals could be: receiving commendations, promotion to y in 2 years, productivity ratings of z, and so on…

Now, create a list of things outside of your control. Instead of trying to not think about them, put them in clear view. This may seem counter-intuitive, especially for somebody who may already be neurotic about such things—but it's not. Here's why creating a list of the uncontrolled helps. First off, it's a list, a physical thing. It allows you to project your fears and insecurities outside of yourself so that you can view them as independent; as mere words or statements on a piece of paper.

Separating your fears from your internal monologue is important. This allows us to view even our deepest insecurities with a more objective perspective. Think about how others would view your list. Would they critique certain fears as realistic and understandable? Would they look at others and shake their heads in disbelief? Would they laugh at how absurd certain fears really are?

Take this opportunity to understand that just because you can't control something, that doesn't mean it is scary, or bad, or dangerous. Understand that many things in life are mysterious for a reason, that we can't possibly know it all, that sometimes there may just be a greater order to the cosmos. Rest assured knowing that if you knew everything, your drive would be dead and your head filled with extraneous information.

Sometimes, ignorance is bliss.

Law 5 - Rejection Leads to Reason

Remember what we said before?

If life always offers us lemons, we'd be sitting around all day making lemonade. Now how the hell are you going to get off your ass and live life if you're always sitting around making lemonade?

The point of this metaphor, of course, is that sometimes life is better with a little adversity. When we are rejected by a partner, rejected by a school, by a job or field, by certain people, denied by certain clubs or places— whatever the form of rejection, getting turned down is a great way to man up.

In fact, getting rejected is one of the main developmental stepping stones for men, especially future alpha males. When we are rejected, man or woman, we learn several things. Firstly, we learn that life is not perfect and neither are we. Secondly, we learn that things will not always go our ways. Thirdly, we learn that opinions differ and behaviors vary. Fourthly, we learn that rejection is potentially advantageous.

Think about it. Not all things in life will align and not all opportunities can be seized. Sometimes people, places and things are not compatible and it's nobody's fault. Sometimes the way of the world allows us to see that one missed opportunity creates another.

Think of it this way: if you don't get what you want, maybe it's a blessing. Take for instance a guy who gets turned down in a job interview. Instead of getting the job and starting next week, he gets depressed about his prospects, heads to the nearest bar, and ends up meeting his future wife. Now, this may seem like a romantic or rare occasion, but it does happen. What's important to remember is simple: you never know where life is taking you. Even if you don't believe in a higher power or grander plan, you can still view rejections in a positive light. If you change your approach or style due to one or more rejections, you may just end up pursuing things you never knew you were good at, having experiences you never knew you'd enjoy, or going places you never imagined you'd be.

Rejection is also evolutionarily important. Our ancestors who were rejected from the tribe faced almost certain death. In the world of hunter/gatherers, the pack-mentality was the survival mentality. Because rejection often led to isolation and death, the human brain developed an aversion to rejection and/or potential rejection. This means that those who feel the most hurt by rejection are those who are most likely to adapt and avoid it in the future. In fact, rejection stimulates the same areas of the brain as physical pain, meaning that the same inclination to avoid physical pain is the inclination that spurs us to avoid emotional suffering.

From rejection, comes reason. Although many of us may act emotionally at first, the best approach is to think rationally. What makes us feel better and more self-assured? Does rejection really ruin us or is it temporary? How can this rejection strengthen you and solidify your resolve? What new chances have opened up as a result? How will you use your resources now so that you can allocate them differently? When did your fear of rejection begin? Is your thinking realistic, or negative?

Do you believe in your ability to change? Do you find that your fear of rejection is based on all-or-nothing thinking? *"What if I lose my job?"* *"What if my partner leaves me?"* *"What if I get sick? What if somebody dies?"* *"What if I have no money?"* *"What if I die?"*

Instead of thinking in terms of black and white (everything is either good or bad), think in terms of grey. Understand that life is a gradient, a spectrum, and there is somebody at literally every conceivable point in that spectrum. Is your fear of rejection leading to future rejections? Are you bringing about self-fulfilling prophecies? Are you acting, thinking and feeling in a way that increases the likelihood of rejection, without even knowing it?

Allow reason to flow from rejection. Assess what went wrong and right. Assess why you felt the way you did before, during and after rejection. Admit what you personally did wrong and what you personally had no control over. Don't beat yourself up. Ask others if you have to, get various opinions from those outside your crazy little head. Don't discount the advantages of rest and relaxation. Remember that you are not failing, you are learning. You are learning what it takes to be better at what you want and/or do. You are learning that life is not a cakewalk, and that it is the tough times that make the good ones so much sweeter.

As many have said, you can't know you're high until you've been low. So treasure the lows. In their own special way, they're just as important as the highs.

Law 6 - You Can't Lose What You've Never Had

This probably isn't what you wanna hear but it's important that somebody says it, so I'll be the one. Firstly, let's start by understanding who we are. Let's start by realizing that life is good and great, and that it is this mind shift, this understanding, that brings us to an important truth:

Fear is all about loss. Consider everything you've ever feared, whether it be monsters under your bed as a kid, or your dwindling paycheck. Whatever makes you quiver, worry or stay up at night, it's probably got something to do with loss. We fear losing ourselves. We fear losing our health, our ability to enjoy all the things we want to do and have to do. We fear losing the ability to care for ourselves and others. We fear losing our position in life. Maybe you have a nice career or are in good social standing, or maybe you've made a lot of cool, interesting friends or have a nice family. Whatever your status, it's probably crossed your mind from time to time what it would be like not to have it. If anybody's ever told you not to "take for granted" what you have, then you know—there's a lot of loss to fear.

Money is another big one. We fear losing a steady stream of income, being unable to pay our bills and afford nice things and amenities like cable television, and iPads, and appliances and cars. We fear losing our retirement, not saving wisely, investing in the wrong things, being swindled, being duped, being lured into a business opportunity that turns out to be a dead-end.

Many people merely fear losing a sense of peace. For those who do not practice mindfulness, sense of peace may be hard to come by. We don't know what to think at times because our mind is moving too fast. Others struggle with keeping their mind in check, with resisting the comforting call of daydreams—and many more are diagnosed with ADHD-PI.

Peace of mind is often tied directly to our sense of loss. If we feel that we've lost too much or have too much to lose, we may seize up. This emotional paralysis can manifest as detachment from everyday life, as depression, and even as irritability or hostility. Some people will try to disguise this problem through substance abuse, but more often than not, there is nothing they can do.

Another sense of loss is that of looks. The cosmetic and plastic surgery industries have made a killing on this. They know that people are naturally insecure about their looks. The main reason is because people want to be received well by others. People also want to receive themselves well. They don't want to look in a mirror and be reminded of the years of stress that have worn on them. They don't want to be reminded that they are going to eventually die.

Basically, everybody fears potential loss, and it is this potential loss that creates issues with everyday living. What one must understand is that there is always potential for loss. In any situation, under any circumstance, something can go wrong. Controlling for this loss is reasonable and expected, but the probability of said loss will never entirely disappear.

Of course, loss is based upon possession. You can't lose that which you don't personally possess. This is why many people get stuck. They feel that if they progress too far they might become too vulnerable. They'll suddenly have something really, really worth having, and losing that something—whether a person, place or thing—can be devastating.

But devastation is not the only outcome. Losing something can lead to gaining something greater. The mere experience of possessing something can be so rewarding, so incredible, that even when that possession ends… the memories will carry on! Again, it all comes back to accepting life as a process, and this can be difficult for people who are crippled emotionally and mentally, or even physically.

When something is lost, sometimes it is for the best. We all grow. We all get older and accrue more experiences and learn more about ourselves and the world. Fearing what we want and need is not right and should never be tolerated. You do not experience life when you fear living!

Go after what you want, and don't think of it as falling flat on your face if you don't get it right away! And once you get it, don't fear losing it!

You know what's more scary than losing something invaluable—than losing some*body* invaluable?

I'll tell you what! Never having had anybody, or anything... because what kind of *person* would ever want that?

Law 7 - Your Greatest Lies are the Ones You Tell Yourself

It's time to wake up.

You need to accept one fact and one fact only. Nobody cares as much about what happens to you as you. You may deny it yourself, you may put on a front, act cool and uncaring, tough and unaffected, selfless and altruistic, but at the end of the day… the only person who *feels* your life is you.

Let me repeat that. Somewhat.
The only person who *loves* your life is you! Other people may feel for you or love you, but they don't experience life as you do. This is because they aren't you (*duh*).

So what you need to do is understand that you—the one in the mirror—are the biggest effect on you. When you do things in your life, you're doing then because you want to and because you need to. You pay your bills because you have to, you go the doctor because you have to and/or want to. You hang out with certain social groups, shop at certain stores, go to certain restaurants, drive on certain roads, take on certain hobbies—because you have decided to do so, whether by want or need.

It's okay to be self-centered. We all are! This doesn't mean that you ignore other people, it just means that you generally strive to do what's best for you. In many cases, that's also what's best or good for others.

This is why you, and you alone, are your biggest critic. But also your biggest friend.

Do you ever struggle with self-love? Do you ever find self-love to be a difficult or seemingly impossible task? Do you want to accept your imperfections, to stop getting in your own way?

If you do, you must realize that the power is in you. Not your family, not your friends, not some expert on T.V., not me (though I'm flattered), and certainly not some junkie behind the Dunkin Donuts.

All these figures may help, but ultimately the decision is up to you. This is why you must treat yourself right. And that begins with honesty.

Be honest with yourself. If you are not achieving what you want, admit. Admit it and move on. Don't sit around sulking, don't ask for help from those unqualified or unwilling to give it, and certainly don't try to avoid your problems through substances or self-destructive behaviors.

Don't lie to yourself. When you lie to somebody else, their perspective of you may change. If they don't know that you're lying, you're going to feel bad at some point—especially if they mean something to you. Even if they don't mean anything to you, you may still feel bad. You may find that you are losing your morals and/or sense of self. You may find yourself caught in a web, unsure what you told one person or another.

Lying to other people can be bad, because even if they don't know it, you're holding something on your chest. And if they do know you're a liar, the damage is even more visible.

But the worst of all—worse than any lie you can tell somebody—is any lie you can tell yourself. When we lie to ourselves, we try to convince ourselves of something we know not to be true. We try to force ourselves into unreal situations or circumstances, we try to be something that seems somehow contrary to our nature, to what we want and need from our lives. When we lie to ourselves, we are also lying to everybody else outside us, because we are deceiving them by being what we are not. There is nothing scarier than a person who is too insecure to *ever* reveal the true self.

And at the end of the day, this is what fear is all about. We fear not being able to be our true selves, to live life with the vision we have in mind, with the people we want and need, with the lifestyle and trajectory that makes us secure.

In order to first conquer our fears—*any* fears—we must first conquer ourselves. You must understand that fear stems not from the external world and its numerous problems and pitfalls, but from your inner world. It is your inner world that allows you to interact with the external. Your thoughts and feelings, attitudes and mindsets, behaviors and output, all *modulate* the external world within the realm of human possibility.

If you can navigate your daily life, aligning both external and internal worlds, then you can navigate even the choppiest of waters. So swim, don't sink; fight, don't flight; make the difference in your life today by becoming the person you want tomorrow.

Day by day, everyday, you can make progress. And with time, and grace, you may just find: your greatest insecurities are also your greatest strengths.

A Special Note:

Thank you for reading *"The Alpha Male: MAN UP and Unlock Your Alpha – An Overnight Guide to Conquering Fear, Women, and Lifelong Success"* If you enjoyed reading this book and would like to be included on an email list for when similar content is available, feel free:

<u>**SUBSCRIBE**</u>

As always, thank you for reading. And may you continue to live healthily and happily.

Sincerely,

<u>C.K. Murray</u>

Other works by C.K. Murray:

1. *<u>Mindfulness Explained: The Mindful Solution to Stress, Depression, and Chronic Unhappiness</u>*

<u>Master the Power of the Unconscious</u>

40. <u>The Alpha Male: MAN UP and Unlock</u>
<u>Your Alpha - An Overnight Guide to</u>
<u>Conquering Fear, Women, and Lifelong</u>
<u>Success</u>